The Art of Prompt Writing

Unlocking AI's Full Potential

By

Emanuel Rose

Copyright © 2024 Emanuel Rose

Published by Emanuel Rose

For more information, please visit www.emanuelrose.com

All rights reserved. No part of this publication may be reproduced, distributed, or transmitted in any form or by any means, including photocopying, recording, or other electronic or mechanical methods, without the prior written permission of the publisher, except in the case of brief quotations embodied in critical reviews and certain other noncommercial uses permitted by copyright law.

Introduction   6

1. Overview of AI in Marketing
   - The rise of AI and its impact on marketing and business strategies.
   - Importance of mastering prompt writing for effective AI utilization.
   - Introduction to the key contributors and their insights.

2. Why Prompt Writing Matters
   - The role of prompt writing in AI content generation.
   - How effective prompts can transform AI outputs from generic to exceptional.
   - The need for curiosity and context in prompt writing.

Chapter 1: Fundamentals of Prompt Writing   10

1. Understanding AI Capabilities
   - Overview of AI models used in marketing and content creation.
   - Differences between generative models and retrieval-augmented generation (RAG) models.

2. Basics of Prompt Writing
   - Defining roles, context, and objectives in prompts.
   - The importance of specificity and clarity in instructions.

3. Common Mistakes to Avoid
   - Overly simplistic prompts.
   - Failing to iterate and refine prompts.
   - Not setting clear expectations for the AI model.

Chapter 2: Structuring Effective Prompts　　　　　　17

1. Components of a Good Prompt
    - Role Designation: Specifying the AI's perspective (e.g., "world-class researcher").
    - Context Setting: Providing background and detailed information.
    - Objective Definition: Outlining the desired outcome and scope.

2. Seeding the Model
    - Techniques for priming AI with relevant information.
    - Using examples and expert inputs to guide the AI's responses.

3. Iterative Refinement
    - Strategies for improving AI outputs through multiple iterations.
    - Analyzing initial outputs and refining prompts for enhanced quality.

Chapter 3: Advanced Prompt Writing Techniques　　27

1. Integrating Emotional Intelligence
    - Embedding emotional nuances in prompts for targeted communication.
    - Utilizing personas and psychological models like DISC and Myers-Briggs in prompt crafting.

2. Prompting for Creativity and Innovation
    - Techniques for encouraging creative AI responses.
    - Using prompts to explore divergent thinking and innovation in content creation.

3. Prompt Engineering for Campaigns
    - Developing prompts for comprehensive marketing campaigns.
    - Creating interconnected content pieces (e.g., blog posts, landing pages, social media).

Chapter 4: Real-World Applications of Prompt Writing   38

1. Case Studies from the Podcast
   - Insights from experts on effective prompt writing.
   - Real-life examples of how prompt writing has been applied in marketing and content strategies.

2. Practical Tips and Tools
   - Recommended AI tools for prompt writing and content generation.
   - Step-by-step guides for using AI tools like ChatGPT, MidJourney, and Descript effectively.

3. Prompt Writing for Different Content Types
   - Crafting prompts for blogs, white papers, social media posts, and email campaigns.
   - Adapting prompt strategies based on content goals and audience.

Chapter 5: Mastering AI for Business Growth   60

1. Leveraging AI for Competitive Advantage
   - Using prompt writing to streamline business processes.
   - Examples of how businesses have successfully integrated AI in operations.

2. Developing AI-Driven Content Strategies
   - Building content pipelines with AI.
   - Creating cohesive and engaging content that aligns with business objectives.

3. Staying Ahead in the AI Revolution
   - Keeping up with the latest AI tools and trends.
   - Resources and communities for ongoing learning and skill development.

Conclusion 71

1. The Future of AI and Prompt Writing
    - Emerging trends in AI and their implications for content creation and marketing.
    - Final thoughts on the evolving role of prompt writing in AI utilization.

2. Resources and Further Reading
    - Books, articles, and courses on AI and prompt writing.
    - Links to podcast episodes and expert interviews featured in the guide.

Appendix A 74

Appendix B 76

About the Author 93

Introduction

Overview of AI in Marketing

The digital marketing landscape is undergoing a radical transformation, driven by the rapid adoption of artificial intelligence (AI) technologies. From automating mundane tasks to generating complex, tailored content, AI is reshaping how businesses connect with their audiences. As these tools become more sophisticated, the way we interact with them must evolve as well. In this era of AI-driven marketing, mastering the art of prompt writing has become a vital skill for anyone looking to harness the true potential of intelligent systems.

While traditional marketing strategies often relied on intuition and manual processes, AI introduces a new paradigm—one that requires precision, clarity, and creativity in communicating with machines. Whether you are developing a content strategy, optimizing digital ads, or engaging customers through chatbots, the quality of your prompts directly impacts the effectiveness of your AI tools. A well-crafted prompt can transform a generic AI response into a highly relevant, actionable output that meets your specific business needs.

This guide, *The Art of Prompt Writing: Unlocking AI's Full Potential*, is designed to be your comprehensive guide to mastering this essential skill.

Drawing insights from leading experts in the field, including thought leaders featured in the *Marketing in the Age of AI* podcast, we will explore the foundational principles of prompt writing and delve into advanced techniques for optimizing AI interactions.

Why Prompt Writing Matters

At its core, prompt writing is about more than just instructing an AI model. It's about leveraging the nuances of language to guide AI systems in producing outputs that are not only accurate but also contextually rich and aligned with your objectives. Just as a skilled director shapes the performance of actors, a well-crafted prompt shapes the performance of an AI, transforming its capabilities from mere automation to intelligent collaboration.

Why does this matter so much? Today's rapidly changing digital environment requires businesses to produce high-quality content quickly and efficiently.

Effective prompt writing allows marketers to generate compelling blog posts, social media content, and email campaigns with unprecedented speed and precision. It enables customer service teams to deliver consistent, high-quality support through AI-powered chatbots. It empowers sales teams to automate outreach and lead generation in a way that feels personalized and authentic.

However, the impact of prompt writing goes beyond marketing. In fields as diverse as healthcare, finance, and education, professionals are using AI to analyze data, create reports, and even predict future trends. In each of these scenarios, the quality of the AI's output depends on the quality of the prompts it receives.

A vague or poorly constructed prompt can lead to irrelevant or even misleading results, while a precise and thoughtful prompt can unlock powerful insights and solutions.

Throughout this guide, you will learn how to craft prompts that make the most of AI's capabilities, transforming it from a simple tool into a powerful partner in your digital strategy. We will begin with the fundamentals—understanding the different types of AI models and how they interpret language. From there, we will explore advanced techniques for structuring prompts that drive creativity and innovation, as well as practical applications across various business scenarios.

By the end of this guide, you will not only have the skills to write effective prompts but also a deeper understanding of how AI can be integrated into your workflows to enhance productivity and creativity. Whether you are a marketer, business leader, or creative professional, this book will equip you with the knowledge and confidence to navigate the AI revolution.

Let's dive in and unlock the full potential of AI through the art of prompt writing.

1
Fundamentals of Prompt Writing

Understanding AI Capabilities

Before diving into the intricacies of prompt writing, it's essential to understand the foundational elements of AI and how it processes language. AI models, particularly those used in marketing and content creation, are designed to interpret and generate human-like text based on the inputs they receive. These models, such as OpenAI's GPT-4 and similar systems, use vast amounts of data to predict and construct meaningful responses.

AI in this context can be broadly categorized into two main types:

1. Generative Models: These models, like GPT-4, are designed to produce text based on a given input. They excel at creating narratives, answering questions, and generating creative content. When you provide a prompt, the model predicts what comes next in the sequence, drawing on its training data to construct responses that align with the input context.

2. Retrieval-Augmented Generation (RAG) Models: RAG models combine the generative capabilities of AI with a database of pre-existing information. This allows them to generate responses that not only create new content but also incorporate specific facts and references. These models are particularly useful for generating detailed reports or content that requires high factual accuracy.

Understanding these differences is crucial because the type of AI model you are working with will influence how you craft your prompts. For instance, a generative model may require more detailed guidance to produce accurate outputs, while a RAG model might benefit from prompts that reference specific data points or topics.

Basics of Prompt Writing

Crafting effective prompts is about setting clear expectations for the AI model. A well-structured prompt includes three key components:

1. Role Designation: Define the role or perspective from which the AI should respond. For example, "Act as a seasoned content strategist" or "Imagine you are a tech-savvy customer service representative." This helps the AI frame its response in a way that aligns with the desired context.

2. Context Setting: Provide background information that will help the AI understand the subject matter and the scope of the response. This might include relevant data, past actions, or specific scenarios. For instance, "Given the recent trends in digital marketing, suggest strategies for increasing engagement among Gen Z users."

3. Objective Definition:

Clearly outline what you want the AI to accomplish. This could range from generating creative ideas to drafting a detailed report. Be specific about the output you expect, such as "Create a 500-word blog post on the benefits of AI in marketing, highlighting three key trends."

By incorporating these elements, you set the stage for the AI to deliver outputs that are aligned with your needs. It's like giving a clear briefing to a team member before they start a project — the more context and direction you provide, the better the results.

Common Mistakes to Avoid

Even with a basic understanding of prompt writing, there are common pitfalls that can lead to unsatisfactory AI outputs. Here are some mistakes to watch out for:

1. Overly Simplistic Prompts: A vague or simplistic prompt, such as "Write a blog post," leaves too much room for interpretation. The AI might generate a response, but it's unlikely to meet your specific needs. Instead, try something more detailed like, "Write a 500-word blog post on the impact of AI on small business marketing, including examples and statistical data."

2. Failing to Iterate and Refine Prompts: It's rare to get the perfect response on the first try. If the initial output isn't what you expected, refine your prompt. Add more context, clarify the objective, or break down the task into smaller parts. For example, instead of "Describe the benefits of using AI in healthcare," you might refine to "List five benefits of using AI in healthcare for improving patient outcomes, focusing on diagnosis and treatment."

3. Not Setting Clear Expectations: If you don't specify the format, tone, or depth of detail you need, the AI's response may not align with your expectations. Be explicit about what you want. For instance, "Provide a 300-word summary of this research article, using an academic tone and avoiding jargon."

These are the foundational aspects of prompt writing. In the next chapter, we will delve deeper into how to structure effective prompts that not only communicate your requirements but also maximize the capabilities of the AI you are working with.

2
Structuring Effective Prompts

Writing an effective prompt is like crafting the blueprint for a building—it defines the structure, scope, and intent of what you want to create. In this chapter, we will explore the essential components of a well-structured prompt, delve into techniques for seeding AI models with the right context, and discuss strategies for refining your prompts through iteration to achieve optimal results.

Components of a Good Prompt

A strong prompt consists of several key elements that work together to guide the AI's response. These components help clarify the role, context, and objectives, ensuring that the output aligns with your specific requirements. Let's break down each element.

1. Role Designation

- **Definition:** Specify the role or perspective from which the AI should respond. This can be anything from a professional role (e.g., "financial analyst") to a specific point of view (e.g., "skeptical reviewer").

- **Example:** "Act as a seasoned marketing strategist and provide a detailed plan to improve brand visibility for a tech startup."

- **Purpose:** Role designation helps the AI frame its responses in a way that is relevant to the context you are targeting. This is particularly useful when you want the output to reflect a specific expertise or tone.

2. Context Setting

- **Definition:** Provide background information or situational details that the AI needs to understand before generating its response. This could include the current market scenario, previous actions, specific data points, or any relevant factors.

- **Example:** "Given that our tech startup recently launched a new SaaS product targeting remote teams, and we are currently focusing on increasing our social media presence, suggest a content strategy that highlights the unique features of our product."

- **Purpose:** Context setting ensures that the AI has all the necessary information to generate an output that is relevant and aligned with the desired context. It reduces ambiguity and increases the precision of the response.

3. Objective Definition

- **Definition:** Clearly outline the expected outcome or goal of the prompt. This includes the type of response (e.g., list, report, analysis), the level of detail, and any specific requirements or constraints.

- **Example:** "Generate a 300-word summary highlighting the key findings of the attached market research report, focusing on trends in consumer behavior for 2024."

- **Purpose:** Defining the objective helps narrow the AI's focus, ensuring that the response meets your specific needs. This reduces the likelihood of receiving irrelevant or overly broad outputs.

By incorporating these components into your prompts, you can guide the AI to produce responses that are not only accurate but also tailored to your unique needs. Next, we'll explore how to seed the model with the right information to further enhance its performance.

Seeding the Model

Seeding involves providing the AI with initial information or examples to guide its response. This is particularly useful when you want to establish a specific tone, style, or format for the output. Effective seeding can transform a generic response into a nuanced and contextually rich piece of content.

1. Using Examples and Precedents

- **Definition:** Provide specific examples or reference materials that the AI can draw from when generating its response.

- **Example:** "Here's an example of a blog post that captures the tone we want: [link to example]. Use this as a guide to create a new post on the benefits of AI in small business marketing."

- **Purpose:** Examples help the AI understand the desired style, structure, and content, making it easier to produce outputs that meet your expectations.

2. Priming with Relevant Data

- **Definition:** Supply the AI with data points, statistics, or specific details that should be included in the response.

- **Example:** "Using the following data, create an infographic summary: 1. 70% of consumers prefer personalized content. 2. AI-driven personalization increases engagement by 30%. 3. Predictive analytics can reduce churn by up to 15%."

- **Purpose:** Priming the AI with relevant data ensures that the response is factually accurate and aligned with the specific information you want to highlight.

3. Defining the Scope and Boundaries

- **Definition:** Set clear boundaries for the AI's response, such as limiting the scope of the content or specifying areas to avoid.

- **Example:** "Write a 500-word article on the future of AI in healthcare. Focus only on predictive diagnostics and exclude discussions on AI in surgery or administration."

- **Purpose:** Defining the scope helps prevent the AI from straying into irrelevant areas, ensuring that the response is concise and on-topic.

Iterative Refinement

Even the best prompts may not produce the perfect output on the first try. Iterative refinement involves reviewing the AI's responses and tweaking the prompt to improve the quality and relevance of the output. This process is crucial for optimizing AI performance, especially for complex or creative tasks.

1. Analyzing Initial Outputs
- Review the AI's initial response to see if it meets your expectations in terms of content, tone, and structure. Identify any gaps, errors, or areas where the response falls short.

2. Adjusting the Prompt
- Based on your analysis, modify the prompt to provide clearer instructions or additional context. For example, if the initial output is too technical, you might adjust the prompt to request a simpler explanation.

3. Testing Variations
- Experiment with different versions of the prompt to see which produces the best results. This might involve changing the role designation, adding new context, or redefining the objective.

4. Refining for Clarity and Specificity

- Ensure that your prompt is as clear and specific as possible. Avoid vague language and be explicit about what you expect from the AI. For example, instead of "Describe the benefits of AI," use "List five benefits of using AI in marketing, with examples from recent case studies."

By applying these strategies, you can iteratively refine your prompts to achieve outputs that closely match your desired outcomes. In the next chapter, we will explore advanced prompt writing techniques, including how to integrate emotional intelligence and creativity into your AI interactions to unlock even greater potential.

3
Advanced Prompt Writing Techniques

Once you've mastered the basics of prompt writing, it's time to explore more advanced techniques. These methods will help you unlock the full potential of AI by going beyond standard responses and crafting outputs that are emotionally intelligent, creative, and highly innovative. In this chapter, we will explore how to integrate emotional intelligence into your prompts, encourage creativity, and leverage prompt writing for complex marketing campaigns.

Integrating Emotional Intelligence

In today's highly personalized marketing landscape, it's not enough for AI to simply respond with facts. In many cases, the output needs to resonate emotionally with the audience. By integrating emotional intelligence into your prompts, you can guide AI to produce responses that align with the psychological and emotional needs of your target audience.

1. Understanding the Role of Emotion in Content

- Emotionally driven content tends to perform better in marketing because it connects on a deeper level with audiences. Whether you're writing a heartfelt customer service email or a persuasive ad campaign, prompting AI to consider emotional tones can enhance the impact of your content.

- **Example Prompt:** "Write a customer apology email that conveys empathy and a genuine desire to resolve the issue. Use a warm, understanding tone that will reassure the customer that their concern is important to us."

2. Utilizing Personas for Targeted Communication

- To craft emotionally intelligent prompts, it's helpful to incorporate personas or psychological models like DISC (Dominance, Influence, Steadiness, Conscientiousness) or Myers-Briggs. These personas allow you to customize the tone and approach for different audience types.

- **Example Prompt:** "Act as a customer service agent writing to a detail-oriented and fact-driven customer (Myers-Briggs: ISTJ). Draft a response that is polite, structured, and offers a step-by-step explanation to resolve the issue."

3. Adjusting Tone Based on Audience Needs

- Emotional intelligence also involves understanding the emotional state of your audience and adapting the tone of your AI's output accordingly. For instance, a frustrated customer requires a different tone than a loyal, satisfied one.

- **Example Prompt:** "Compose a thank-you email to a long-time customer. Express sincere appreciation and include a personalized offer as a reward for their loyalty. Use a friendly and appreciative tone."

By integrating emotional intelligence into your prompts, you can ensure that the AI's responses are not only informative but also empathetic and aligned with your audience's emotional needs.

Prompting for Creativity and Innovation

AI can be a powerful tool for generating creative ideas and fostering innovation in content creation. However, creativity doesn't always come naturally to AI, as it relies on the prompts you give it to explore new ideas and possibilities. Here are techniques to encourage more innovative outputs.

1. Open-Ended Prompts for Divergent Thinking

- To encourage creative thinking, use open-ended prompts that allow AI to explore a range of possibilities rather than limiting it to one specific answer.

- **Example Prompt:** "Brainstorm 10 unconventional ways to use AI in content marketing that have not yet become mainstream."

- **Purpose:** This type of prompt invites the AI to generate multiple ideas, often leading to more innovative and less predictable outputs.

2. Scenario-Based Prompts

- Placing the AI in a hypothetical scenario encourages it to think creatively within specific constraints. This is particularly useful for exploring future trends, new products, or untested strategies.

- **Example Prompt:** "Imagine you are leading the marketing team for a futuristic tech company in 2030. What three major trends would you capitalize on to engage the market, and how would you adjust your content strategy to reflect these trends?"

- **Purpose:** Scenario-based prompts challenge the AI to think forward and apply its knowledge to a new context, often resulting in more innovative strategies.

3. Combining Disparate Ideas

- Creativity often arises from the intersection of seemingly unrelated ideas. By asking AI to combine different concepts, you can push it to generate more innovative responses.

- **Example Prompt:** "Create a unique marketing strategy that blends gamification techniques with influencer marketing to drive brand awareness among Gen Z."

- **Purpose:** This type of prompt encourages the AI to synthesize multiple ideas into a novel approach, sparking creativity that traditional prompts might not elicit.

By crafting prompts that encourage open-ended exploration, scenario thinking, and the combination of different concepts, you can use AI to produce creative and innovative content that sets your brand apart.

Prompt Engineering for Campaigns

As marketing strategies become more complex, AI can assist in managing and generating content for multi-channel campaigns. However, to make the most of AI in this context, you need to design prompts that guide it to produce consistent, interconnected outputs across different platforms.

1. Creating Cohesive Multi-Platform Content

- Multi-platform campaigns require a consistent voice, but the content itself must adapt to each platform's format and audience. Craft prompts that instruct AI to generate content tailored to various platforms while maintaining overall thematic consistency.

- **Example Prompt:** "Create a 500-word blog post introducing our new AI-driven analytics tool. Then, generate a series of 5 social media posts (2 for LinkedIn, 2 for Twitter, 1 for Instagram) that highlight key features and benefits. Ensure each post is adapted to the platform's format and audience."

- **Purpose:** This prompt helps the AI produce a range of content that is cohesive in messaging but tailored to the nuances of each platform.

2. Driving Engagement with Sequential Prompts

- Campaigns often require content that builds on previous materials, such as a series of emails, blog posts, or social media updates. Sequential prompts guide the AI to create interconnected pieces that lead the audience through a narrative or sales funnel.

- **Example Prompt:** "Write a three-email drip campaign introducing a new online course. The first email should focus on building awareness and interest, the second on addressing common questions, and the third on offering a limited-time discount. Ensure each email logically follows from the previous one."

- **Purpose:** Sequential prompts help the AI produce content that not only delivers isolated messages but builds a continuous and engaging flow across multiple touchpoints.

3. Creating Personalized Content at Scale

- AI can be used to generate personalized content for different segments of your audience. This requires prompts that instruct the AI to adapt messaging based on the unique needs, preferences, or behaviors of each segment.

- **Example Prompt:** "Generate two versions of a product announcement email. One version should be targeted at first-time buyers, emphasizing ease of use and introductory offers. The second version should target repeat customers, focusing on loyalty rewards and advanced features of the product."

- **Purpose:** By crafting prompts that segment content by audience type, you can use AI to deliver more personalized and relevant messaging at scale.

By leveraging AI for campaign content, you can streamline the process of producing cohesive, multi-platform strategies and ensure that your messaging remains consistent and engaging across all customer touchpoints.

4

Real-World Applications of Prompt Writing

Now that we've explored the foundational and advanced techniques of prompt writing, it's time to see how these skills are applied in real-world scenarios. This chapter will highlight case studies from various industries, practical tips and tools for effective prompt writing, and tailored strategies for different content types. These examples will demonstrate how prompt writing can drive success in marketing, customer service, content creation, and beyond.

Case Studies from the Podcast

In the *Marketing in the Age of AI* podcast, several experts provided valuable insights into the practical use of prompt writing in real-world scenarios.

These case studies, based on the episodes featuring Jonathan Green, West Stringfellow, Jeff Borschowa, and Vince Warnock, showcase how AI can be harnessed to solve complex business challenges, generate high-quality content, and drive innovation. Below are detailed examples of how each expert has applied AI to optimize processes and achieve business growth.

Jonathan Green: Enhancing Customer Profiling and Content Creation with AI

Jonathan Green, an e-commerce strategist, shared how AI can be an invaluable tool in identifying ideal customer profiles and creating content that resonates with those customers. Many businesses struggle with the initial step of determining their ideal customer, often leading to ineffective marketing strategies.

Jonathan explained how AI can streamline this process by using iterative prompts to gather relevant data and refine customer profiles.

One of Jonathan's key insights was the need to "activate" AI's advanced capabilities by framing prompts that encourage multi-step, two-way conversations. For instance, by asking the AI, "I want to figure out who my ideal customer is. What information do you need from me?", the user invites the AI to ask clarifying questions. This reduces cognitive load and allows the AI to lead the user through the customer profiling process more efficiently.

- **Example Prompt:** "I want to figure out who my ideal customer is. What information do you need from me? Ask me one question at a time."

  - **Context:** This prompt initiates a structured conversation, enabling AI to ask for specific details about the user's target market, customer preferences, and pain points. By gathering this data step-by-step, the AI builds a comprehensive customer profile, which can be used to create personalized marketing campaigns.

Jonathan also discussed the importance of using AI as a **collaborative partner**. In one example, he shared how framing the AI as a co-participant in problem-solving can generate better results. For instance, asking the AI, "We're going to work on a project together. I'll tell you what I need, and you'll ask questions until we figure out the best way to accomplish this," turns the AI into an active participant in decision-making.

- **Example Prompt:** "We're going to work on a project together. I'm going to tell you what I need, and you'll ask me questions until we figure out the best way to accomplish this."

  - **Context:** This approach allows for a less structured but more iterative problem-solving process, where the AI adjusts its strategy based on continuous feedback from the user. It fosters a dynamic exchange where both parties work toward refining solutions.

Jonathan also advocated for using **one-shot or multi-shot examples** to teach the AI a user's tone or writing style. For instance, he shared how feeding the AI previous examples of his emails helped the system replicate his style in future content creation tasks.

- **Example Prompt:** "Here are the last 25 short emails I wrote. Use these to understand my structure and tone, and then generate a new email following this style."

  - **Context:** By providing the AI with multiple examples, users ensure that the content generated mirrors their voice, tone, and formatting preferences, allowing for more personalized and consistent output.

Jonathan's use of **iterative prompting**—refining AI's output by providing feedback — is a cornerstone of effective AI utilization. By viewing AI as a junior employee who needs guidance, users can continually improve the content it produces.

- **Example Prompt:** "Rewrite this response in a friendlier tone, keeping the message concise."

    - **Context:** This prompt allows users to fine-tune the AI's output, adjusting tone, structure, or word choice to fit their specific needs. This iterative process ensures that the final content aligns with the brand's voice and messaging.

West Stringfellow: Using AI to Build Competitive Advantage and Accelerate Business Strategy

West Stringfellow, an innovation strategist, focused on how AI could be used to gather competitive intelligence, improve customer engagement, and accelerate business strategy. His emphasis on **multi-shot prompting** provided a framework for how AI could generate increasingly accurate insights by building on previous information.

West recommended using AI to analyze business and customer data holistically, incorporating behavior patterns, competitor insights, and market conditions. By feeding the AI multiple sources of data, users can generate more strategic growth options.

- **Example Prompt:** "Upload all business data and customer information (excluding personal identifiable information). Use this data to analyze current market opportunities and provide five growth strategies based on customer behavior and competitor trends."

  - **Context:** This prompt allows AI to analyze customer data, helping businesses identify potential growth areas. The AI assesses current customer behavior and competitor strategies to suggest actionable insights for long-term planning and development.

Another key use case West highlighted was AI's role in **competitive intelligence**. By uploading competitor websites and job listings, businesses can gain a detailed understanding of their rivals' strategies, pricing models, and upcoming product focuses. AI speeds up a process that traditionally took weeks to complete.

- **Example Prompt:** "Analyze this competitor's website (URL provided) and generate insights about their pricing strategy, technology stack, and product differentiation. Based on recent job listings, predict their upcoming product focus."

    - **Context:** This prompt directs the AI to analyze key elements of a competitor's business, offering insights that can inform the company's strategic response. Understanding a competitor's strengths and weaknesses helps businesses stay ahead in the market.

West also spoke about using AI to **build a competitive moat**, allowing businesses to deepen their customer relationships through personalized engagement strategies. By analyzing customer feedback and behavior, AI can recommend tailored strategies to improve customer loyalty.

- **Example Prompt:** "Use AI to evaluate our customer feedback data. Identify key areas where we can enhance customer experience and create a deeper connection with our user base. Suggest three personalized engagement strategies."

  o **Context:** This prompt allows AI to identify patterns in customer feedback, helping businesses strengthen their relationship with customers by addressing their specific needs. Personalized strategies make it harder for competitors to disrupt the market share.

West also encouraged businesses to see AI as a **continuous thought partner** in strategic planning. By interacting with AI throughout a product development cycle, businesses can refine their strategies and adapt to changing conditions in real-time.

- **Example Prompt:** "We're launching a new product next year. Act as a thought partner and guide us through the development process, from market analysis to product launch strategy. Ask follow-up questions as needed and adjust the strategy based on new data."

  - **Context:** This prompt fosters ongoing collaboration with AI, where the system provides continuous feedback and guidance throughout the product lifecycle. This real-time adaptability allows businesses to refine their strategies on the go, ensuring that they remain relevant and responsive to market changes.

Jeff Borschowa: Automating Content Creation and Marketing Funnels with AI

Jeff Borschowa, a consultant specializing in AI for small businesses, emphasized the need to provide AI with detailed context and iterative feedback to generate high-quality outputs. He particularly focused on how AI could help automate **content creation** and **build marketing funnels** efficiently.

Jeff highlighted the importance of **role assignments** in prompting AI to generate expert-level results. By assigning a specific role to the AI, such as "world-class expert in healthcare innovations," users can ensure that the AI tailors its output to match professional standards.

- **Example Prompt:** "You are a world-class expert in writing Harvard case studies. Help me write a white paper using the Harvard methodology."

  - **Context:** This prompt directs the AI to follow the formal, well-established framework of Harvard case studies. Assigning expertise to the AI results in more structured, high-quality content.

Jeff also stressed the importance of **iterative prompting** to refine outputs. The first response from AI is often imperfect, so users must guide it through multiple iterations to improve the content's accuracy and relevance.

- **Example Prompt:** "Now that we've discussed the initial white paper ideas, can you identify the world's top experts in this field? Focus on those with publications in medical journals."

    - **Context:** By continuously refining the prompt, the AI can filter out irrelevant or generalized data and focus on expert-level information, improving the final product.

Jeff provided an example of using AI to **build a complete marketing funnel** in a single conversation. Starting with content creation, the AI can generate landing pages, email campaigns, and social media posts, all aligned with the same project.

- **Example Prompt:** "You are a landing page expert with a background in SEO. Create a landing page outline to promote our white paper on healthcare AI innovations. Focus on keywords and a strong call-to-action."

  - **Context:** This approach allows users to generate interconnected marketing assets without needing to start each component from scratch. The AI retains context, helping to build cohesive campaigns efficiently.

Vince Warnock: Humanizing Content and Automating Social Media with AI

Vince Warnock, a digital marketing expert, discussed how AI can help small businesses generate high-quality visual and written content that feels human. One of his key insights was about the importance of making AI-generated content sound less robotic, which can be achieved by explicitly instructing the AI to avoid overly formal or mechanical language.

- **Example Prompt:** "Write a follow-up email for a customer inquiry. Use a fun, friendly, and journalistic tone. Ensure it doesn't sound like it was written by AI."

    o **Context:** This prompt directs AI to use a conversational tone, avoiding the rigid, formal structures that sometimes characterize AI-generated text. By explicitly instructing the AI to "sound human," users can create more engaging and personable content.

Vince also explained how AI could be used to automate complex social media workflows, allowing influencers and small business owners to produce a significant amount of content without sacrificing quality.

- **Example Prompt:** "Create a blog post about the power of established museums like the Louvre and their influence on modern design. Pull three to five supporting sources from the last month and generate a related image."
    - **Context:** This prompt shows how AI can automate content creation by generating a blog post, gathering supporting sources, and creating an accompanying image—all in one go. This dramatically speeds up the content production process, freeing up time for more strategic tasks.

Practical Tips and Tools for Effective Prompt Writing

To make the most of prompt writing, it's essential to use the right tools and techniques. Here are some practical tips and recommended tools to help you refine your prompt writing skills and achieve optimal outcomes.

1. Use AI Writing Assistants for Rapid Prototyping

- Tools like ChatGPT, Jasper, and Writesonic are excellent for quickly generating content prototypes based on your prompts. Experiment with different prompt structures and observe how small changes can lead to varying outputs.

- **Tip:** Start with broad prompts to see the range of responses, then refine your prompt based on the initial outputs to get closer to the desired result.

2. Incorporate Contextual Data with Retrieval Tools

- For more complex projects, tools like Perplexity.ai and Frase.io can help you integrate contextual data into your prompts, making the AI's responses more fact-based and relevant.

- **Tip:** Use these tools to include up-to-date information or specific data points in your prompts. For example, "Using the latest market data from 2023, write a report on emerging trends in digital marketing."

3. Leverage Pre-Trained Models for Specific Tasks

- Tools like Descript for podcast editing and Lumen5 for video creation are pre-trained to handle specific content types. Use them to guide the AI in generating high-quality, purpose-built content.

- **Tip:** For video scripts, try prompts like, "Write a 60-second video script introducing our new product line, focusing on eco-friendly features and targeting a millennial audience."

4. Track Performance and Iterate

- Use analytics tools to measure the effectiveness of your AI-generated content. Track metrics such as engagement rates, conversion rates, and feedback from your audience to determine what works and what doesn't.

- **Tip:** Regularly review these metrics and adjust your prompts accordingly. For example, if a blog post isn't generating expected traffic, refine the prompt to include more targeted keywords or adjust the tone to better fit your audience.

Prompt Writing for Different Content Types

The application of prompt writing varies significantly depending on the type of content you are creating. Here, we'll explore tailored strategies for some common content types:

1. Blog Posts

- **Strategy:** For blog posts, focus on providing a clear structure and specifying the tone, audience, and key points you want to cover.

- **Example Prompt:** "Write a 1,000-word blog post on the future of AI in digital marketing. Include an introduction, three main sections on emerging trends, ethical considerations, and practical applications, and a conclusion that provides actionable advice for marketers."

2. White Papers and Reports

- **Strategy:** Use prompts that guide the AI to produce content that is research-focused, data-driven, and well-structured. Include references to credible sources.

- **Example Prompt:** "Draft a 2,000-word white paper on the impact of AI on supply chain management. Include an overview of current challenges, how AI is addressing these challenges, and case studies from three major industries. Use recent data and cite credible sources."

3. Social Media Posts

- **Strategy:** Social media requires concise, engaging, and visually appealing content. Tailor your prompts to generate short-form content that includes hooks, hashtags, and calls-to-action.

- **Example Prompt:** "Create a series of three Instagram posts promoting our upcoming webinar on AI in marketing. Use an engaging hook, include relevant hashtags, and encourage followers to register through the link in bio."

4. Email Campaigns

- **Strategy:** For emails, prompts should focus on personalization, clear messaging, and strong calls-to-action. Segment your audience and create prompts that address the specific needs of each group.

- **Example Prompt:** "Write a welcome email for new subscribers to our AI newsletter. Introduce our company, highlight the benefits of subscribing, and include a link to our latest blog post on AI trends."

By applying these tailored strategies to your prompt writing, you can optimize AI-generated content for a variety of formats and ensure that your messaging resonates with your audience.

5
Mastering AI for Business Growth

As businesses continue to integrate AI into their operations, the potential for growth and innovation is immense. However, the effectiveness of AI-driven strategies hinges on how well these systems are directed through prompt writing. In this chapter, we will explore how businesses can leverage prompt writing to gain a competitive edge, develop effective AI-driven content strategies, and navigate the challenges of an AI-dominated landscape. By mastering these techniques, you can use AI not only as a tool for efficiency but also as a driver of business growth.

Leveraging AI for Competitive Advantage

AI is transforming industries by enabling businesses to automate processes, personalize customer interactions, and make data-driven decisions with unprecedented speed and accuracy. To fully harness these benefits, businesses need to understand how to strategically apply AI through effective prompt writing.

1. Streamlining Business Processes

- **Automating Routine Tasks:** Many businesses struggle with time-consuming administrative tasks that can be automated using AI. By crafting precise prompts, you can instruct AI tools to handle everything from scheduling to data entry, freeing up human resources for higher-level strategic activities.

- **Example Prompt:** "Using the data from the last quarter's sales reports, generate a weekly performance summary that highlights key trends, identifies top-performing products, and suggests areas for improvement. Present this information in a two-page document with charts and bullet points."

2. Enhancing Customer Experience

- **Personalized Interactions:** Customer service and marketing teams can use AI to provide personalized experiences at scale. By using prompt writing to create customized responses based on user behavior and preferences, businesses can increase customer satisfaction and loyalty.

- **Example Prompt:** "Generate a personalized email response for a customer inquiry about product availability. Use a friendly tone, address the customer by name, and include a list of alternative products if the requested item is out of stock. Mention the estimated restock date if applicable."

3. Data-Driven Decision Making

- **Predictive Analytics and Insights:** Businesses can use AI to analyze large datasets and extract actionable insights. By crafting prompts that guide the AI in performing detailed analyses, companies can gain deeper insights into market trends, customer behavior, and operational performance.

- **Example Prompt:** "Analyze the sales data from the past year and identify three major trends in customer purchasing behavior. Include a breakdown of seasonal variations, product preferences, and demographic factors that influence sales."

4. Boosting Marketing Effectiveness

- **Targeted Campaigns:** AI can help marketers design and execute highly targeted campaigns. Using advanced prompt writing techniques, marketers can create customized messaging and content that resonates with specific audience segments, thereby increasing engagement and conversions.

- **Example Prompt:** "Create a segmented email campaign for our new product launch. Write three versions of the email: one targeting first-time buyers, one for returning customers, and one for high-value clients. Each email should highlight the product's benefits relevant to each group and include a personalized call-to-action."

By leveraging AI in these ways, businesses can not only streamline operations but also gain a competitive advantage by responding more quickly and effectively to market changes and customer needs.

Developing AI-Driven Content Strategies

An effective content strategy is crucial for building brand awareness, engaging customers, and driving sales. AI can play a significant role in developing and executing these strategies, but only if guided by well-crafted prompts. Here's how you can use prompt writing to optimize your content strategy.

1. Creating a Content Pipeline

- **Automating Content Creation:** AI can help automate the creation of blog posts, social media updates, and even long-form content like white papers. By setting up a structured content pipeline with specific prompts, you can ensure a steady flow of high-quality content.

- **Example Prompt:** "Generate a monthly content calendar for our blog, including 12 post titles and brief outlines for each. Focus on topics related to AI in marketing, customer success stories, and practical tips for using AI tools. Ensure a mix of how-to guides, case studies, and thought leadership pieces."

2. Optimizing Content for SEO and User Engagement

- **SEO-Friendly Content:** AI can assist in optimizing content for search engines by generating keyword-rich articles that align with current SEO trends. Using prompts that specify keyword usage, meta descriptions, and internal linking strategies can help improve content visibility.

- **Example Prompt:** "Write a 1,000-word blog post on 'How AI is Transforming Customer Service.' Include the keywords 'AI in customer service,' 'chatbots,' and 'customer experience.' Use subheadings and bullet points for readability, and include internal links to our related articles on AI and customer engagement."

3. Dynamic Content Personalization

- **Tailoring Content to Audience Segments:** AI can help deliver personalized content to different audience segments based on their preferences and behavior. By crafting prompts that specify content variations for each segment, you can create a more personalized user experience.

- **Example Prompt:** "Create two versions of a landing page for our AI analytics tool. The first version should target small business owners, highlighting ease of use and affordability. The second version should target enterprise clients, focusing on scalability, advanced features, and ROI."

4. Content Performance Analysis and Optimization

- **Monitoring and Adjusting Strategy:** Use AI to track content performance metrics such as engagement, conversion rates, and audience feedback. By setting prompts that guide AI to analyze these metrics, you can continuously refine your content strategy.

- **Example Prompt:** "Analyze the performance of our last 10 blog posts. Identify the top three posts in terms of traffic and engagement. Provide insights on what contributed to their success and suggest three new topics based on these insights."

With AI-driven content strategies guided by effective prompt writing, businesses can create a robust content ecosystem that engages audiences, builds brand authority, and drives measurable results.

Staying Ahead in the AI Revolution

The digital landscape is rapidly evolving, and staying ahead requires a proactive approach to integrating AI into your business strategy. This involves not only mastering prompt writing but also keeping up with the latest tools, trends, and best practices.

1. Adopting New AI Tools and Technologies

- As new AI tools and platforms emerge, they offer additional capabilities for automating and enhancing business processes. Regularly explore and adopt new technologies that align with your business goals.

- **Tip:** Follow industry news and join AI-focused communities to stay informed about the latest developments. Experiment with new tools in a controlled environment before integrating them into your core business processes.

2. Ongoing Skill Development

- The skills required to work effectively with AI are constantly evolving. Investing in training and development for yourself and your team is crucial to maintaining a competitive edge.

- **Tip:** Enroll in courses on AI and prompt writing, attend workshops, and participate in webinars. Encourage your team to do the same and share their learnings.

3. Building a Data-Driven Culture

- To fully leverage AI, it's important to foster a data-driven culture within your organization. This involves using data and AI insights to inform decision-making across all levels of the business.

- **Tip:** Implement regular data reviews and encourage team members to use AI-generated insights to guide their strategies and projects.

4. Ethical Considerations and Compliance

- As AI becomes more integrated into business operations, ethical considerations such as data privacy and bias must be addressed. Ensure that your use of AI complies with legal standards and ethical guidelines.

- **Tip:** Develop a clear AI ethics policy for your organization and provide training on responsible AI usage. Regularly review and update your practices to stay compliant with evolving regulations.

By staying ahead of the curve and continuously evolving your AI strategies, you can position your business to thrive in an increasingly competitive and AI-driven world.

Conclusion

The Future of AI and Prompt Writing

As we've explored throughout this guide, prompt writing is a powerful skill that can transform how we interact with AI, unlocking its full potential in various aspects of business and marketing. The future of AI is bright, and as these technologies continue to evolve, so too will the techniques and strategies for effective prompt writing. Staying ahead in this rapidly changing field requires not only mastering the current best practices but also remaining curious and adaptable as new developments emerge.

This means that the role of prompt writers will become even more critical, as crafting effective prompts will require a deeper understanding of the nuances of language, audience psychology, and the specific needs of each business context.

Another key trend is the growing integration of AI into more aspects of business and daily life. From predictive analytics and personalized content delivery to advanced customer service solutions, AI is becoming an indispensable tool across industries. As a result, the demand for skilled prompt writers who can guide these systems effectively will continue to rise. By honing your skills now, you'll be well-positioned to take advantage of the opportunities that come with this expanding field.

One of the most exciting trends on the horizon is the increasing sophistication of AI models, which will be able to understand and generate more nuanced and contextually aware responses.

The Evolving Role of Prompt Writing

Prompt writing is no longer just about giving instructions to a machine; it's about shaping the future of how we interact with technology. It's a blend of art and science that requires creativity, analytical thinking, and an understanding of human behavior. As AI becomes more integrated into our lives, the ability to communicate effectively with these systems will be a valuable skill for professionals in all fields.

This guide has provided a comprehensive guide to mastering the art of prompt writing, from the fundamentals to advanced techniques and real-world applications.

Whether you're looking to enhance your marketing efforts, streamline business operations, or simply understand AI better, the skills you've learned here will help you achieve your goals.

But this is just the beginning. The landscape of AI and prompt writing will continue to evolve, presenting new challenges and opportunities. By staying informed and continuously improving your skills, you can remain at the forefront of this exciting field and make a significant impact on your business and beyond.

Appendix A: Additional Resources for AI and Prompt Writing Mastery

To continue mastering AI and prompt writing, we've curated a list of essential resources. These include books, podcasts, and tools that dive deeper into AI, content marketing, and prompt engineering.

Whether you're looking for practical insights, thought leadership, or advanced strategies, the following resources will help you enhance your understanding and skills in the evolving world of AI-driven marketing.

Books & Guides

Authentic Marketing in the Age of AI by Emanuel Rose
A comprehensive guide on leveraging AI in modern marketing strategies.
View the book here

AI Prompt Hack by Emanuel Rose
A detailed resource for refining prompt writing and optimizing AI outputs.
Explore the AI Prompt Hack

Generative Engine Optimization (GEO) by Emanuel Rose
Insights into the future of digital marketing with Generative Engine Optimization.
Learn about GEO

Content Marketing Trends
Stay ahead with the latest trends and strategies in content marketing.
Explore Content Marketing Trends

Podcast Episodes

**Marketing in the
Age of AI Podcast**
Featuring expert discussions on the latest in AI and marketing.
Explore the podcast

**Episode: Vince Warnock
on Capturing AI in Marketing**
Watch on YouTube

**Episode: Jeff Borschowa
on Mastering Prompt
Engineering**
Watch on YouTube

**Episode: West Stringfellow
on AI Strategy and
Competitive Advantage**
Watch on YouTube

**Episode: Jonathan Green
on Customer Profiling and
Content Creation**
Watch on YouTube

Articles & Tools

**AI Marketing Tools
& SaaS Directories**
A curated list of AI tools and SaaS directories for efficient content marketing.
Browse AI Marketing Tools

Emanuel Rose Blog
Explore a variety of articles on AI, marketing strategies, and prompt writing by Emanuel Rose.
Read the blog here

Appendix B: Customizable AI Prompts for Practical Application

In this appendix, we've compiled a list of general prompts based on the examples provided throughout the guide. These prompts are designed to be flexible and adaptable for various business and content creation needs. By using these general prompts as templates, you can tailor them to suit your specific objectives, whether you're crafting marketing content, optimizing workflows, or driving creative output with AI.

The goal of this appendix is to empower you to build on the foundations of prompt writing discussed in the previous chapters, enabling you to unlock the full potential of AI in your unique context. Each prompt can be customized by adjusting the key elements, allowing you to guide AI effectively in producing outputs that align with your goals.

Feel free to experiment with these prompts, refine them to suit different scenarios, and integrate them into your ongoing AI-driven strategies.

Example Prompt: "Act as a seasoned content strategist and provide a detailed plan to improve brand visibility for a tech startup."
General Prompt: "Act as a [specific role/expert] and provide a detailed plan to improve [objective] for a [type of business]."

Example Prompt: "Given that our tech startup recently launched a new SaaS product targeting remote teams, and we are currently focusing on increasing our social media presence, suggest a content strategy that highlights the unique features of our product."
General Prompt: "Given that [business/product description], suggest a [type of strategy] that highlights [specific focus/feature]."

Example Prompt: "Generate a 300-word summary highlighting the key findings of the attached market research report, focusing on trends in consumer behavior for 2024."
General Prompt: "Generate a [specific length] summary highlighting the key findings of the [attached document], focusing on [specific focus/trend]."

Example Prompt: "Here's an example of a blog post that captures the tone we want: [link to example]. Use this as a guide to create a new post on the benefits of AI in small business marketing."
General Prompt: "Here's an example of [content type] that captures the tone we want: [link to example]. Use this as a guide to create new content on [specific topic]."

Example Prompt: "Using the following data, create an infographic summary: 1. 70% of consumers prefer personalized content. 2. AI-driven personalization increases engagement by 30%. 3. Predictive analytics can reduce churn by up to 15%."
General Prompt: "Using the following data, create a [content type]: [data points]."

Example Prompt: "Write a 500-word article on the future of AI in healthcare. Focus only on predictive diagnostics and exclude discussions on AI in surgery or administration."
General Prompt: "Write a [specific length] article on [topic]. Focus only on [specific sub-topic] and exclude discussions on [other sub-topics]."

Example Prompt: "List five benefits of using AI in marketing, with examples from recent case studies."
General Prompt: "List [number] benefits of [specific topic], with examples from [sources/case studies]."

Example Prompt: "Write a customer apology email that conveys empathy and a genuine desire to resolve the issue. Use a warm, understanding tone that will reassure the customer that their concern is important to us."
General Prompt: "Write a [type of email/message] that conveys [emotion], and use a [specific tone]."

Example Prompt: "Act as a customer service agent writing to a detail-oriented and fact-driven customer (Myers-Briggs: ISTJ). Draft a response that is polite, structured, and offers a step-by-step explanation to resolve the issue."
General Prompt: "Act as a [specific role] writing to a [audience type/personality type]. Draft a response that is [tone/style] and includes [specific requirements]."

Example Prompt: "Brainstorm 10 unconventional ways to use AI in content marketing that have not yet become mainstream."
General Prompt: "Brainstorm [number] unconventional ways to [specific task], focusing on ideas that are not yet mainstream."

Example Prompt: "Compose a thank-you email to a long-time customer. Express sincere appreciation and include a personalized offer as a reward for their loyalty. Use a friendly and appreciative tone."
General Prompt: "Compose a [type of message] to a [audience type]. Express [specific emotion], and include [special offer/incentive]. Use a [specific tone]."

Example Prompt: "Create a unique marketing strategy that blends gamification techniques with influencer marketing to drive brand awareness among Gen Z."
General Prompt: "Create a [type of strategy] that blends [technique 1] with [technique 2] to achieve [specific objective] among [target audience]."

Example Prompt: "Imagine you are leading the marketing team for a futuristic tech company in 2030. What three major trends would you capitalize on to engage the market, and how would you adjust your content strategy to reflect these trends?"

General Prompt: "Imagine you are [role/position] in [scenario]. Identify [number] major trends you would capitalize on, and explain how you would adjust your [specific strategy]."

Example Prompt: "I want to figure out who my ideal customer is. What information do you need from me? Ask me one question at a time."

General Prompt: "Help me figure out [specific goal]. Ask me questions one at a time to gather the information you need."

Example Prompt: "Create a 500-word blog post introducing our new AI-driven analytics tool. Then, generate a series of 5 social media posts (2 for LinkedIn, 2 for Twitter, 1 for Instagram) that highlight key features and benefits. Ensure each post is adapted to the platform's format and audience."

General Prompt: "Create a [specific length] blog post introducing [product/service]. Then, generate [number] social media posts for [platforms], highlighting key features and benefits."

Example Prompt: "Write a three-email drip campaign introducing a new online course. The first email should focus on building awareness and interest, the second on addressing common questions, and the third on offering a limited-time discount. Ensure each email logically follows from the previous one."

General Prompt: "Write a [number]-email drip campaign introducing [product/service]. The first email should focus on [specific focus], the second on [specific focus], and the third on [specific focus]. Ensure logical flow between emails."

Example Prompt: "Generate two versions of a product announcement email. One version should be targeted at first-time buyers, emphasizing ease of use and introductory offers. The second version should target repeat customers, focusing on loyalty rewards and advanced features of the product."

General Prompt: "Generate [number] versions of a [specific email type]. One version should target [audience type 1], focusing on [specific emphasis], and the second version should target [audience type 2], focusing on [specific emphasis]."

Example Prompt: "We're going to work on a project together. I'm going to tell you what I need, and you'll ask me questions until we figure out the best way to accomplish this."
General Prompt: "We're going to work on [specific project] together. I'll provide instructions, and you'll ask questions to help figure out the best approach."

Example Prompt: "Here are the last 25 short emails I wrote. Use these to understand my structure and tone, and then generate a new email following this style."
General Prompt: "Here are [number] examples of my [content type]. Use these to understand my [style/structure], and then generate a new [content type] following this approach."

Example Prompt: "Rewrite this response in a friendlier tone, keeping the message concise."
General Prompt: "Rewrite this [content type] in a [specific tone], keeping the message [concise/clear]."

Example Prompt: "Upload all business data and customer information (excluding personal identifiable information). Use this data to analyze current market opportunities and provide five growth strategies based on customer behavior and competitor trends."
General Prompt: "Use [data type] to analyze [specific focus], and provide [number] strategies based on [specific factors/trends]."

Example Prompt: "Analyze this competitor's website (URL provided) and generate insights about their pricing strategy, technology stack, and product differentiation. Based on recent job listings, predict their upcoming product focus."
General Prompt: "Analyze [competitor's information] and generate insights about their [specific focus]. Predict [specific outcome] based on [relevant data]."

Example Prompt: "You are a world-class expert in writing Harvard case studies. Help me write a white paper using the Harvard methodology."
General Prompt: "You are a world-class expert in [specific expertise]. Help me write [content type] using [methodology/style]."

Example Prompt: "Use AI to evaluate our customer feedback data. Identify key areas where we can enhance customer experience and create a deeper connection with our user base. Suggest three personalized engagement strategies."
General Prompt: "Use [data type] to evaluate [specific focus]. Identify key areas for improvement and suggest [number] strategies to enhance [specific goal]."

Example Prompt: "Now that we've discussed the initial white paper ideas, can you identify the world's top experts in this field? Focus on those with publications in medical journals."
General Prompt: "Identify the world's top experts in [specific field]. Focus on those with [specific credentials/publications]."

Example Prompt: "We're launching a new product next year. Act as a thought partner and guide us through the development process, from market analysis to product launch strategy. Ask follow-up questions as needed and adjust the strategy based on new data."
General Prompt: "Act as a thought partner for [specific project]. Guide us through the process from [starting point] to [ending point], asking follow-up questions and adjusting the strategy based on new data."

Example Prompt: "You are a landing page expert with a background in SEO. Create a landing page outline to promote our white paper on healthcare AI innovations. Focus on keywords and a strong call-to-action."
General Prompt: "You are a [specific role] with expertise in [specific area]. Create [content type] to promote [product/service], focusing on [specific elements]."

Example Prompt: "Write a follow-up email for a customer inquiry. Use a fun, friendly, and journalistic tone. Ensure it doesn't sound like it was written by AI."
General Prompt: "Write a [specific message] using a [specific tone]. Ensure it [specific requirement, such as avoiding an AI-sounding response]."

Example Prompt: "Create a blog post about the power of established museums like the Louvre and their influence on modern design. Pull three to five supporting sources from the last month and generate a related image."

General Prompt: "Create a [content type] about [topic]. Pull [number] supporting sources from [specific time frame] and generate a related [media type]."

Example Prompt: "Generate a monthly content calendar for our blog, including 12 post titles and brief outlines for each. Focus on topics related to AI in marketing, customer success stories, and practical tips for using AI tools. Ensure a mix of how-to guides, case studies, and thought leadership pieces."

General Prompt: "Generate a [specific time frame] content calendar for [platform], including [number] post titles and outlines. Focus on topics related to [specific areas]. Ensure a mix of [content types]."

Example Prompt: "Write a 1,000-word blog post on 'How AI is Transforming Customer Service.' Include the keywords 'AI in customer service,' 'chatbots,' and 'customer experience.' Use subheadings and bullet points for readability, and include internal links to our related articles on AI and customer engagement."

General Prompt: "Write a [specific length] blog post on [topic]. Include the keywords [specific keywords], use subheadings and bullet points for readability, and include internal links to [related content]."

Example Prompt: "Create two versions of a landing page for our AI analytics tool. The first version should target small business owners, highlighting ease of use and affordability. The second version should target enterprise clients, focusing on scalability, advanced features, and ROI."

General Prompt: "Create [number] versions of [content type] for [specific product/service]. The first version should target [audience type 1], focusing on [specific focus], and the second version should target [audience type 2], focusing on [specific focus]."

Example Prompt: "Create a segmented email campaign for our new product launch. Write three versions of the email: one targeting first-time buyers, one for returning customers, and one for high-value clients. Each email should highlight the product's benefits relevant to each group and include a personalized call-to-action."

General Prompt: "Create a segmented [content type] for [specific product/service]. Write [number] versions, each targeting [audience types]. Highlight benefits relevant to each group and include a personalized call-to-action."

Example Prompt: "Analyze the performance of our last 10 blog posts. Identify the top three posts in terms of traffic and engagement. Provide insights on what contributed to their success and suggest three new topics based on these insights."

General Prompt: "Analyze the performance of [specific content]. Identify the top [number] based on [performance metrics]. Provide insights on their success and suggest [number] new topics based on these insights."

Example Prompt: "Using the data from the last quarter's sales reports, generate a weekly performance summary that highlights key trends, identifies top-performing products, and suggests areas for improvement. Present this information in a two-page document with charts and bullet points."

General Prompt: "Using [specific data], generate a [time frame] performance summary that highlights [specific focus]. Present this information in [specific format]."

Example Prompt: "Generate a personalized email response for a customer inquiry about product availability. Use a friendly tone, address the customer by name, and include a list of alternative products if the requested item is out of stock. Mention the estimated restock date if applicable."

General Prompt: "Generate a [message type] for [specific inquiry]. Use a [tone], address the recipient by name, and include [specific details/alternatives]."

Example Prompt: "Analyze the sales data from the past year and identify three major trends in customer purchasing behavior. Include a breakdown of seasonal variations, product preferences, and demographic factors that influence sales."

General Prompt: "Analyze [data type] from [specific time frame] and identify [number] major trends in [specific focus]. Include a breakdown of [specific elements]."

Example Prompt: "Draft a 2,000-word white paper on the impact of AI on supply chain management. Include an overview of current challenges, how AI is addressing these challenges, and case studies from three major industries. Use recent data and cite credible sources."

General Prompt: "Draft a [specific length] white paper on [topic]. Include an overview of [specific focus], and case studies from [number] major [industries/sectors]. Use [specific data] and cite [credible sources]."

Example Prompt: "Write a 1,000-word blog post on the future of AI in digital marketing. Include an introduction, three main sections on emerging trends, ethical considerations, and practical applications, and a conclusion that provides actionable advice for marketers."

General Prompt: "Write a [specific length] blog post on [topic]. Include [number] main sections on [specific focus areas], and a conclusion that provides [specific outcome/advice]."

Example Prompt: "Write a welcome email for new subscribers to our AI newsletter. Introduce our company, highlight the benefits of subscribing, and include a link to our latest blog post on AI trends."

General Prompt: "Write a [message type] for [audience type]. Introduce [company/product], highlight [specific benefits], and include a link to [related content]."

Example Prompt: "Create a series of three Instagram posts promoting our upcoming webinar on AI in marketing. Use an engaging hook, include relevant hashtags, and encourage followers to register through the link in bio."

General Prompt: "Create a series of [number] [content type] promoting [event/product]. Use an engaging hook, include [specific elements like hashtags], and encourage [desired action]."

About the Author

Emanuel Rose was born and raised on the West Coast of the United States. He has spent over three decades earning a reputation in cutting-edge marketing. A renowned expert in the field, Emanuel specializes in branding, advertising, and day-to-day operations at his digital agency, Strategic eMarketing. His passion lies in helping companies achieve business success from the bottom to the top.

Emanuel's unique approach to marketing strategies has resulted in countless clients reaching their goals.

Emanuel enjoys learning his craft and implementing new techniques and theories for his clients, not only in his home state of Oregon, but around the world. Together with his hand-selected staff, Emanuel creates opportunities while solving challenges in the ever-changing digital landscape. He is a firm believer in using his personal experiences to help others and this dedication continues to impress.

Not to be outdone on the digital battlefields, Emanuel is an avid outdoorsman. He feels connected to the planet wandering the towering forests or absorbing the energy pouring in from the ocean. His childhood fantasy of discovering those special places translates to his writings. The freedom and joy in exploring the natural world is a welcome addition to his life.

strategicemarketing.com

More Marketing Books by Emanuel Rose

Emanuel Rose, a seasoned marketing expert, offers a diverse collection of books designed to equip marketers with the knowledge and strategies needed to thrive in the ever-evolving landscape of modern marketing.

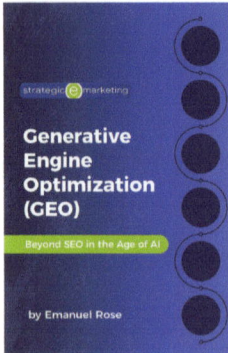 

Generative Engine Optimization (GEO)

In the Generative AI-driven world, traditional SEO is no longer enough. This book takes digital marketing to the next level, leveraging artificial intelligence to optimize content for AI-driven search engines. This guide reveals the cutting-edge techniques and strategies you need to stay competitive in a rapidly evolving landscape.

Packed with practical tips, case studies, and step-by-step instructions, this book is your essentil guide to thriving in the age of AI.

Content Marketing Trends

From leveraging niche content to embracing data-driven insights, this book is your roadmap to content marketing success in the AI era. Learn how to:

- Build a loyal community around your brand
- Optimize your content for search engines and social algorithms
- Elevate your brand through strategic podcast guesting and hosting
- Assemble your content marketing tech stack

Authentic Marketing in the Age of AI

Authentic Marketing in the Age of AI is a guide for marketers looking to create effective marketing strategies in the era of AI. It covers topics such as understanding authentic marketing, the impact of AI on marketing, building authentic marketing strategies, engaging customers authentically, measuring the effectiveness of marketing efforts, overcoming challenges, and leveraging AI tools. It provides practical insights and strategies for marketers to stay ahead of the curve and achieve marketing success in the age of AI.

Authenticity: Marketing to Generation Z

Emanuel dives into the demographics of Generation Z and explores successful marketing campaigns that hit the bullseye with this generation. He guides readers through the process of developing a fully-fledged marketing plan and web presence that will make them a pro at reaching both Business to Business (B2B) and Business Consumer (B2C) campaigns. With his extensive experience in marketing, Emanuel offers practical insights and actionable strategies for businesses to achieve marketing success in the digital age.

Raise More, Reach More

Raise More, Reach More is a guide to unleash the power of innovative fundraising and lead your non-profit to success. This ground-breaking guide is tailored explicitly for executive directors, marketing professionals, and all those involved in nature restoration, adventure programming, and child-centered nature initiatives.

The Social Media Edge

The Social Media Edge is a guide for executives to leverage the social CEO, employee advocacy, and social media to boost their brand image. The book covers topics such as understanding the role of emplouee advocacy, the social CEO phenomenon, building a social media advocacy program for employees, creating content, best practices, measuring success, and success stories. It also provides insights on developing effective content strategies, using paid social ads, and internal communications, creating a social media policy, analyzing, and optimizing performance, and using video to enhance employee advocacy.